Please God…

Don't Let Me Become a Bag Lady!

Aunti Says

Published by ProRisk Press

Box 253, Alberta Beach, Alberta Canada T0E 0A0

Patricia@auntisays.com

Patriciaogilvie.com

ISBN 978-0-9780520-8-9

Revised Second Edition Series Printing 2016

"Money alone sets all the world in motion."

DEDICATION

This extraordinary coloring book is inspired by and dedicated to young and old aspiring to successfully manage money and life around the world. The series is dedicated to my family.

ACKNOWLEDGMENT

To my husband and biggest supporter enabling us to live a financial stress free lifestyle.

To my teachers and examples throughout life, who have been integral parts of my financial growth. I love and appreciate you all.

To all my clients, past, present and future, who have allowed me to touch their lives. Without you, I wouldn't have written this inspirational book.

And to the close friends who confided they were scared to death of having nothing, living off the street and becoming bag ladies. I heard you.

INTRODUCTION

What if life beats out a path that drags you into screaming nightmares every night, waking cold, wet, alone and scared.

What if you don't have a penny to your name?

What if you are so hungry you eat bugs and grubs crawling in the dirt around you?

What if your worst nightmare comes true – you're all alone, a stinky bag lady with knots in your hair and nothing to show for your life?

The good news is, it's only a dream and doesn't need to come true, ever. You can stop that thought process now.

Now you can color your way out of financial distress and rebuild your self- confidence, daily.

Nothing is more satisfying that focusing on what you do want to achieve in life. And what better way than to spend minutes and even hours on a single thought process: coloring a desired image keeps you in a relaxed state of Zen.

Your focus and mind stay rooted to positive thoughts. You are using proven stress-relief coloring skills, those same skills that inhibit nightmares, and produce more alpha and beta waves of calming energy.

The first of its kind, this coloring book is for you, the adult woman who finds herself alone from divorce or widowed, stressed about her financial future, or married and worried about money. You now have a tool to help ease frustrations and begin to explore creativity, mindfulness and help strengthen your focus on the good.

God answers.

You won't become a bag lady — ever. Grab your colored pencils, pens or crayons. You're about to develop a focus on what you want and keep your confidence level intact.

I've Got the Power

I've got the power, yes I do
To make hearts turn and mine too.
Listen to me and you will hear
Whatever your imagination holds, have no fear.

My words are glib, but never glum
And powerful are they
So won't you come?
While I weave the web
And make you think
Of the power I've got
The power to sink
Your heart in mine
And back again.

'Cause the powers' in the word,
And that's fine.
Fine for me and fine for you
All I want is your mind and heart too!

Plus, you get to add anything else you want to this little book. It's yours to play in, think in, and make shifts that you are truly appreciated and loved. You are strong inside and out.

Color the words. Color the mandalas and the pictures. Write in the margins. And know this: you are special and appreciated.

Enjoy because

Aunti Says

I know if I save, I could stop worrying about my future. If I don't, I continue to worry.

It's time to quit worrying and put a bit aside every week.

A woman without money is like a she-wolf without teeth.

Today I will stop gumming my way through life!

Up to now, my reward of a thing well done is to have done it. Next, I will be paid.

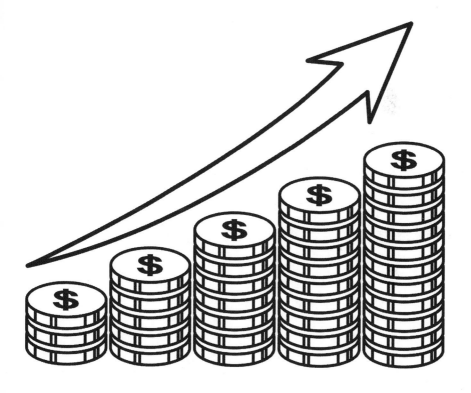

If I go to bed at night believing I will fail, for sure I will. Tonight I tell myself before I fall asleep that when I awake, I will be reminded I am a success.

I cannot always control what is going on around me, but I can sure control what I think about what is going on around me. I have appreciation for my surroundings.

I intend to get so fixated on what I want, that I drown out any vibration or reverberation that has anything to do with what I do not want. I climb on my broomstick and decide where I'm flying.

I have little to no security unless I can live bravely, and imaginatively when I choose a challenge instead of just plain ole competence. I am ready to carve out a plan. Here's the start of my list of what I want.

I know in my heart things can change to something new, to something strange. I know it.

To relax my brain, I will color swirls to get my creative flow.

Life is always a tightrope or a feather bed. Give me the tightrope. - Edith Wharton

Thanks Edith... but my tightrope is heavy with crap! So let's deal with my crap first, OK?

My C.R.A.P.
Write your C.R.A.P. here:

Conflicts: eg: I hate work but I need money

Resistances: eg: I could work for myself

Anxieties: eg: I will be an old bag lady!

Problems: eg: I eat out too much

Things happen to me!
Good things, like a
new love, bad things
like a job loss. Now I
will change my mind
about the C.R.A.P.
And move into
S.N.A.P. I will list
contingency plans
and save for the
unexpected. It's time.

My S.N.A.P.
Write your S.N.A.P. here:

Satisfactions: eg: I will be happier at work

New Thinking: eg: I can work for myself

Appreciations: eg: I love myself as I am

Promises I Keep: eg: I will eat at home

I may be disappointed if I fail, but I am doomed if I don't at least try.

I want a new car. What color? What make? Hmmm let's try it.

I also know I can never be stronger than when I arm myself with my own strengths and even weaknesses.

I don't need someone else to fix me.

I still want a loving, caring, long-term relationship with me!

God loves me.

God loves me.

God loves me.

The universe is change; my life is what my thoughts make it.

God Loves Me.

Life begins at the end of my comfort zone.

I want to travel and see some beautiful new places.

I will save money to go.

I have learned over the years that when my mind is made up, I feel less fear and I have courage to take a step. I will be okay.

I saved some money today. I think I will treat myself.

Wait! How about sock it away instead for down the road?

That definitely feels better.

It is only possible to live happily ever after on a day-to-day basis. A man's best friend can demonstrate being present in each moment. I love a pup!

I enjoy my ideas, and thoughts. It's important that I leave all others opinions out of my head. They've got their own game going on; it's not mine and mine isn't theirs. Stop asking others what they think.

It's my birthday. Before I may be tempted to spend a fortune on a gift and celebration, I do remember that it's not the trappings nor splendor, but introspections and tranquility which bring me happiness.

There is nothing in the world more peaceful to the mind than the smell of rich earth mingled with the scent of blossoms.

A garden is a beauty and a mystery, just like me.

Now that my mind is still, I will go to that "catch-all" closet where all my impulse buying is hidden and clear it out. I will keep what I need and give away what I don't. Clear my conscience and my karmic bank account.

I don 't have to be married to renew my financial vows. I will rethink my relationship with money and write out a commitment for myself and even my partner so we can begin making our lives debt free.

I sometimes think shopping is therapeutic, but I will find different ways to relieve stress. Exercise? Cook? At least I'm not buying restaurant meals. Sing? Swim? Ride my bike? Learn bongos. Bongos!

Take stock. I open my wallet and see how many credit cards. Are they free and clear of charges? No? Then I need to pay off the biggest one first and stop spending until they are clear. Heal my brain.

Holidays are here.
And that means gifts
and spending I don't
have for everything.
What to Do?

I'll throw a party
instead as a gift for
my friends and family.
That covers everyone
and they will love it.

Work for myself, from home: full-time, part-time, a second job? Help reduce my debts. Now to find a space in my home to work from because I can write off up to 50% of my Internet, utilities, rent and more. Feels good.

If I am a first time homeowner, and I see the price of houses skyrocket, what to do? Condo. Let it appreciate, and then eventually sell it for a new house.

I have this bad habit of spending every day on something. I will commit to NO spending one day this week. Which day? Tuesday. Instead I will color this mandala.

I can't always see my debt as real, So today I will create a paper chain made with links colored as $100 bills and make it as long as my credit card debt. Then as I pay down, I will remove one link each time and feel awesome knowing I am in control.

I did it! Lot's of thinking, changing my mind and making commitments to reduce and erase debt. Congratulations to me. Now I must remember not to get complacent. Revise my plan regularly, ask God for insights and list everything. Great job ME!

No matter how much I make or even how much I spend, there is still only ONE rule. Always, always, always sock 10% away into savings and investments. I love to be surprised.

I will never think again I could be a Bag Lady!

"Money alone sets all the world in motion."

Thank You for Being Here!

If you like this little purse sized adult coloring book, you'll love the 2nd and 3rd Adult Coloring Books in this Trilogy of stress reducers and fun increasers.

Look for Marbles and Respect in the Series here:

Www.auntisays.com/shop/

Made in the USA
Charleston, SC
12 June 2016